Zen Seeds, Empty Mind

By Yanir Harel "Gong Shim"

EMP Empty Mind Publishing House

www.emptymind-publishing.com

First edition 2012

Published by EMP Empty Mind Publishing House
All rights reserved by the author Yanir Harel

ISBN 13: 978-1-4781-8079-1

Library of Congress Control Number: 203900331
CreateSpace Independent Publishing Platform, North Charleston, SC

Printed in the U.S.A.

No part of this book may be reproduced or transmitted in any form or by any means, electronic or mechanical, including all recording, information storage, copying and retrieval possibilities, without written permission from the author.

About the Author

The author ("Gong Shim") is an unassuming, respected spiritual teacher. Yanir was born in Italy in December, 1971. Yanir learned with the Kwan Um School of Zen and experienced the traditions of Theravada Buddhism and Soto Zen.

Yanir's direct and sincere teaching style, clearly recognizable in these pages, is to point directly to the truth. After fourteen years of guiding numerous students, Yanir decided to write this clear companion, which encourages people to seek their true self and points to the right direction.

To my beloved ones, Nicole and Amy.
Walk with a smile and a clear mind or your entire life will be only a dream.

Thank you, Nicole, for your wisdom and patience.
Thank you, Amy, for pointing to the truth.

CONTENTS

Foreword		*11*
First Seed	What are you?	*15*
Second Seed	Empty Mind	*21*
Third Seed	Practice	*27*
Fourth Seed	Compassion	*33*
Fifth Seed	Moment World	*39*
Sixth Seed	Thinking Words	*45*
Seventh Seed	The Diamond Sword	*51*
Parting Thoughts		*59*
The Great Heart of Wisdom Sutra		*60*
The Gateless Gate		*63*
The Meditation Posture and Breathing Exercise		*64*

FOREWORD

Inside this book you will find seeds derived from the wisdom tree of Zen Buddhism. You will find teaching seeds and practice seeds. These seeds hold many gifts to be taken, and they are all for you.

These seeds have a special quality. This quality manifests itself while you read the words in this book. When you read these words, they become one with you and will go everywhere with you.

One day they will help you see a special place. Sometimes we call this place the Buddha world, but actually it will be your world. Just let yourself truly see it. These seeds will guide you well.

It is said that there is actually no gate to the path of the Buddha and that following this path lets you walk the earth freely. So what's holding you back?

THE FIRST SEED

What Are You?

THE FIRST SEED

What Are you?

Have you ever thought about it?

Really, can you tell what you are?

René Descartes said, "I think therefore I am," but what are you before thinking begins? What are you before you use words? What are you before you have ideas?

Truly, what are you before you start explaining yourself?

Let me tell you a secret: there is a special place that exists before words and ideas. You just can't give a name to it.

So, what are you?

It's okay to have a little doubt in your heart.
Maybe you'll discover that you simply do not know the answer.

Not knowing is actually a good place.
So hold on to this mind that doesn't know.

It will help you discover your true mind.

THE SECOND SEED

Empty Mind

THE SECOND SEED

Empty Mind

In this world we like to do a lot of thinking. Sometimes our thoughts are so strong that we do things that we later regret. Try doing something different. Allow yourself not to think. You might be surprised to discover that it is a liberating experience. Rest assured; it is possible to exist without thinking.

Now try it for real.

Try to keep an empty mind for one minute. Here's how:

Close your eyes and don't think about anything. Set an alarm clock in order to take time without being distracted. If a thought arises in your mind, focus on your breathing and let the thought dissolve. Just feel the sensations that emerge from your body. Later you will also learn the practice of the Diamond Sword.

Could you do it?

If you found it difficult, just continue reading.

THE THIRD SEED

Learn the True Meaning of

Practice

THE THIRD SEED

Learn the true meaning of

Practice

This is a very interesting seed, one which needs to be handled with great care. It is a reminder that you must learn to make use of the words in this book.

The words on these pages are only small black ink symbols, but they also point to some real action to be taken.

In your life, you may come across many teaching words. However, these words are usually lost, forgotten shortly after they have been read.

Don't just read and forget. Use the seeds in this book and see the place to which they are pointing. Don't worry; the seeds will guide you to the right path.

When you truly use the seeds, you will become one with them. Then your mind will open and you'll be able to throw these pages away. But before you do that, try practicing a bit.

THE FOURTH SEED

Compassion

THE FOURTH SEED

Compassion

Not for others but for yourself.

Some people always run to help others but they never stop to help themselves.

Compassion toward others is good, but first you must learn to help yourself. Only then will you truly be able to help others.

Learn to forgive yourself when you fail.
Learn to love yourself even when you are wrong.
This is the true way of compassion.
Do these things for yourself and it will also help others.

Compassion for yourself will enable you to endure times of hardship in life, and one day you will be able to help someone else.

Remember this seed as you continue reading.

THE FIFTH SEED

Moment World

THE FIFTH SEED

Moment World

Everything around us is always changing.
Your body changes as it grows older. Ideas change. Substance changes. Situations change. Fortune changes.

Everything changes.

As you read these words, the paper they are printed on ages and your body undergoes change.

Everything in the substance world around you changes.

If you open your mind, you will see that the past is already gone. The future is yet unknown. The only true place that is left is the present, but even the present is not enough.

Life is what happens to you moment after moment. This is a wonderful place to be and we call it Moment World. Actually, it's the ability to sense the flow of moments, which is the flow of change. For a moment, try not to worry about past deeds or the future. Put all your energy into this moment. This could be the best moment of your life, and you could have another one right after the first. Eventually, you will come to see that everything around us is just this one wonderful moment.

Try it. Just feel this moment.

THE SIXTH SEED

Thinking Words

THE SIXTH SEED

Thinking Words

When you see something, you don't really see it. As you open your eyes, words immediately jump into your head in order to describe the object you see.

We are so used to words that we let them create a strange world. It is the world of words. Yet the world existed before words came into being.

It seems that now it's words that control us. Words were once our servants, but now they have taken a strong hold over us.

Try to return to the world before words. It's easy. Just open your mind and regain your true sight. Stop thinking in words and take a fresh look at the world.

We like to say that words are just a vessel. Once you've reached your destination, you can leave it and enjoy a nice walk.

Have fun. Try to look at the world without describing it.

Just try it.

To help you see the world without words, continue and experience the Diamond Sword.

THE SEVENTH SEED

The Diamond Sword

THE SEVENTH SEED

The Diamond Sword

The teaching of the Diamond Sword is an ancient one. It is a secret that has been handed down from teacher to student for centuries. It is a simple teaching, yet one of great efficacy.

STEP I

To hold the Diamond Sword, you must first learn to breathe properly.

Stand up straight. Close your eyes. Gently expand your diaphragm and let the air fill your lungs. Gently retract your diaphragm and let the air flow out. Feel the flow of air inside your body. Relax your body. Feel the flow of energy inside you with every breath you take.

STEP II

Imagine a sword with a transparent diamond blade.

The sword awaits your command. You will operate this sword, and nothing can hinder your command.

STEP III

When a thought enters your mind, order your sword to cut it. When the sword cuts a thought, the thought disappears.

You must cut through all thoughts, even the thought that says that you are doing well. Cut everything, leaving your mind empty of all thoughts and pictures. Many demons and desires will appear, but you must cut through them all with your diamond sword.

STEP IV

Try cutting through thoughts for five minutes.

You can do this standing, sitting, or lying down. Just do it whole-heartedly. After a while you can use a cutting word. Just think of the word "katz" when a thought arises. Katz cuts through the thought.

STEP V

Learn to appreciate your mind when it's empty. Be fully alert at every moment. Experience everything around you but without thinking about it.

STEP VI

Extend the amount of time you let your mind stay empty.

STEP VII

Make this practice a habit, and the true world will appear before you. You will be truly amazed.

When you practice this, you will come to understand the true meaning of the diamond sword. Thinking about it will not help you. You have to just do it.

THE LAST STEP

The sword is used to cut through wild weeds and through your demons. But after some time, you will have to drop the sword. We like to say that you are now sitting on your sword. If a thought arises in your mind, just be aware of it, and after a while it will disappear. Then let yourself just be. Awake in a place before words. Keep returning to this place and you will grow stronger.

This is your true self, and yet this is only the beginning.

Parting Thoughts

There are so many words, but none of them can help you if you don't get to know the mind that exists before words. For this you have received the gift of these seeds. Don't turn down this gift.

The water of life must be taken, or your entire life will be only a dream.

Once you attain your true mind, you will have a new direction in life.

"How can I help you?" One day you will find yourself asking someone this very question. On that day, you will know that your life has reached its true purpose.

Katz

If you'd like to read more teaching words, you can read the following chapters: "**Great Heart of Wisdom Sutra,**" "**The Gateless Gate,**" *and* "**The Meditation Posture and Breathing Exercise.**" *Try to read them after practicing the Diamond Sword. Only then will you see the true meaning behind the words.*

The Great Heart of Wisdom Sutra

Avalokiteshvara Bodhisattva, while practicing deep *Prajna Paramita* ("the wisdom of going beyond"), perceived that all five *skandhas* ("forms, feelings, perceptions, impulses, and consciousness") were empty and was thus saved from suffering and distress.

Shariputra:

Form is no different than emptiness.
Emptiness is no different than form.
That which is form is emptiness.
That which is emptiness is form.
Feelings, perceptions, impulses, consciousness—the same is true of these.

Shariputra:

All dharmas ("teachings") are marked with emptiness.
They do not appear or disappear,

are not tainted or pure,
do not increase or decrease.
Therefore in emptiness there is no form,
no feelings, no perceptions, no impulses, no consciousness,
no eyes, no ears, no nose, no tongue, no body, no mind,
no color, no sound, no smell, no taste, no touch, no object
of mind,
no realm of eyes, and so forth until no realm of mind
consciousness,
no ignorance, and also no extinction of ignorance,
and so forth until no old age and no death and no extinction
of old age and death,
no suffering, no origination, no stopping, no path,
no cognition, also no attainment;
with nothing to attain,
the Bodhisattva depends upon Prajna Paramita,
and his mind is no hindrance;
without any hindrance no fear exists;
far apart from every inverted view,

he dwells in Nirvana.

All buddhas in the three worlds

depend on Prajna Paramita

and attain complete, unsurpassed enlightenment.

Therefore know the Prajna Paramita

is the great transcendent mantra,

is the great bright mantra,

is the utmost mantra,

is the supreme mantra,

which is able to relieve all suffering

and is true, not false.

So proclaim the Prajna Paramita mantra;

proclaim the mantra that says,

"Gone, gone, gone beyond, gone all the way beyond, Bodhi Svaha!"

"Gate, gate, paragate, parasamgate, Bodhi svaha!"

The Gateless Gate

The great way has no gate.

A thousand roads enter it.

When you pass through this gateless gate, you freely walk between heaven and earth.

So I am asking you: What is holding you back from walking freely between heaven and earth?

The Meditation Posture and Breathing Exercise

From the teaching words of Kaiten Nukariya*:

"There are two postures in Zazen—that is to say, the crossed-leg sitting, and the half crossed-leg sitting. Seat yourself on a thick cushion, putting it right under your haunch. Keep your body so erect that the tip of the nose and the navel are in one perpendicular line, and both ears and shoulders are in the same plane. Then place the right foot upon the left thigh, the left foot on the right thigh, so as the legs come across each other. Next put your right hand with the palm upward on the left foot, and your left hand on the right palm with the tops of both the thumbs touching each other. This is the posture called the crossed-leg sitting. You may simply place the left foot upon the right thigh, the position of the hands being the same as in the cross-legged sitting. This posture is named the half crossed-leg sitting. You can also start by putting your legs in any comfortable position.

"Do not shut your eyes; keep them always open during the whole Meditation. Do not breathe through the mouth; press your tongue against the roof of the mouth, putting the upper lips and teeth together with the lower.... Breathe rhythmically through the nose, keeping a measured time for inspiration and expiration. Count for some time either the inspiring or the expiring breaths from one to ten, then beginning with one again. Concentrate your attention on your breaths going in and out as if you are the sentinel standing at the gate of the nostrils. If you do some mistake in counting, or be forgetful of the breath, it is evident that your mind is distracted....

"Breathing exercise is one of the practices of Yoga, and

somewhat similar in its method and end to those of Zen. Yogi Ramacharaka shows how modern Yogis practice it: '(i) Stand or sit erect. Breathing through the nostrils, inhale steadily, first filling the lower part of the lungs, which is accomplished by bringing into play the diaphragm, which, descending, exerts a gentle pressure on the abdominal organs, pushing forward the front walls of the abdomen. Then fill the middle part of the lungs, pushing out the lower ribs, breastbone, and chest. Then fill the higher portion of the lungs, protruding the upper chest, thus lifting the chest, including the upper six or seven pairs of ribs. In the final movement the lower part of the abdomen will be slightly drawn in, which movement gives the lungs a support, and also helps to fill the highest part of the lungs. At the first reading it may appear that this breath consists of three distinct movements. This, however, is not the correct idea. The inhalation is continuous, the entire chest cavity from the lower diaphragm to the highest point of the chest in the region of the collar-bone being expanded with a uniform movement. Avoid a jerking series of inhalations, and strive to attain a steady, continuous action. Practice will soon overcome the tendency to divide the inhalation into three movements, and will result in a uniform continuous breath. You will be able to complete the inhalation in a couple of seconds after a little practice. (ii) Retain the breath a few seconds. (iii) Exhale quite slowly, holding the chest in a firm position, and drawing the abdomen in a little and lifting it upward slowly as the air leaves the lungs. When the air is entirely exhaled, relax the chest and abdomen. A little practice will render this part of exercise easy, and the movement once acquired will be afterwards performed almost automatically.'

"The Yogi breathing above mentioned is fit rather for physical exercise than for mental balance, and it will be beneficial if you take that exercise before or after Meditation. Japanese masters mostly bold it very important to push forward. The lowest part of the abdomen during Zazen, and they are right so far as the present writer's personal experiences go.

"If you feel your mind distracted, look at the tip of

the nose; never lose sight of it for some time, or look at your own palm, and let not your mind go out of it, or gaze at one spot before you. This will greatly help you in restoring the equilibrium of your mind. Chwang Tsz thought that calmness of mind is essential to sages, and said: 'The stillness of the sages does not belong to them as a consequence of their skilful ability; all things are not able to disturb their minds; it is on this account that they are still. When water is still, its clearness shows the beard and eyebrows (of him who looks into it). It is a perfect level, and the greatest artificer takes his rule from it. Such is the clearness of still water, and how much greater is that of the human spirit? The still mind of the sage is the mirror of heaven and earth, the glass of all things.

"Forget all worldly concerns, expel all cares and anxieties, let go of passions and desires, give up ideas and thoughts, set your mind at liberty absolutely, and make it as clear as a burnished mirror. Thus let flow your inexhaustible fountain of purity, let open your inestimable treasure of virtue, bring forth your inner hidden nature of goodness, disclose your innermost divine wisdom, and waken your Enlightened Consciousness to see Universal Life within you.

'Zazen enables the one,' says Kei-zan, 'to open up his mind, to see his own nature, to become conscious of mysteriously pure and bright spirit, or eternal light within him.'

"Once you become conscious of Divine Life within, you can see it in your brethren, no matter how different they may be in circumstances, in abilities, in characters, in nationalities, in language, in religion, and in race. You can see it in animals, vegetables, and minerals, no matter how diverse they may be in form, no matter how wild and ferocious some may seem in nature, no matter how unfeeling in heart some may seem, no matter how devoid of intelligence some may appear, no matter how insignificant some may be, no matter how simple in construction some may be, no matter how lifeless some may seem. You can see that the whole universe is Enlightened and penetrated by Divine Life.

"Zazen is a most effectual means of destroying selfishness, the root of all sin, folly, vice, and evil, since it enables us to see that every being is endowed with divine spirituality in common with men. It is selfishness that throws dark shadows on life, just as it is not the sun but the body that throws shadow before it. It is the self-same selfishness that gave rise to the belief in the immortality of soul, in spite of its irrationality, foolishness, and superstition. Individual self should be a poor miserable thing if it were not essentially connected with the Universal Life. We can always enjoy pure happiness when we are united with nature, quite forgetful of our poor self. When you look, for example, into the smiling face of a pretty baby, and smile with it, or listen to the sweet melody of a songster and sing with it, you completely forget your poor self at that enraptured moment. But your feelings of beauty and happiness are for ever gone when you resume yourself, and begin to consider them after your own selfish ideas. To forget self and identify it with nature is to break down its limitation and to set it at liberty. To break down petty selfishness and extend it into Universal Self is to unfetter and deliver it from bondage. It therefore follows that salvation can be secured not by the continuation of individuality in another life, but by the realization of one's union with Universal Life, which is immortal, free, limitless, eternal, and bliss itself. This is easily affected by Zazen....

"The beatitude of Zen is Nirvana, not in the Hinayanistic sense of the term, but in the sense peculiar to the faith. Nirvana literally means extinction or annihilation; hence the extinction of life or the annihilation of individuality. To Zen, however, it means the state of extinction of pain and the annihilation of sin. Zen never looks for the realization of its beatitude in a place like heaven, nor believes in the realm of Reality transcendental of the phenomenal universe, nor gives countenance to the superstition of Immortality, nor does it hold the world is the best of all possible worlds, nor conceives life simply as blessing. It is in this life, full of shortcomings, misery, and sufferings that Zen hopes to realize its beatitude.

"It is in this world, imperfect, changing, and moving, that Zen finds the Divine Light it worships. It is in this phenomenal universe of limitation and relativity that Zen aims to attain to highest Nirvana. 'We speak,' says the author of Vimalakirtti-nirdeca-sutra, 'of the transitoriness of body, but not of the desire of the Nirvana or destruction of it.' 'Paranirvana,' according to the author of Lankavatarasutra, 'is neither death nor destruction, but bliss, freedom, and purity.' 'Nirvana,' says Kiai Hwan, 'means the extinction of pain or the crossing over of the sea of life and death. It denotes the real permanent state of spiritual attainment. It does not signify destruction or annihilation. It denotes the belief in the great root of life and spirit.' It is Nirvana of Zen to enjoy bliss for all sufferings of life. It is Nirvana of Zen to be serene in mind for all disturbances of actual existence. It is Nirvana of Zen to be in the conscious union with Universal Life or Buddha through Enlightenment.

"Nature offers us nectar and ambrosia every day, and everywhere we go the rose and lily await us. 'Spring visits us men,' says Gu-do, 'her mercy is great. Every blossom holds out the image of Tathagata.' 'What is the spiritual body of Buddha who is immortal and divine?' asked a man to Ta Lun (Dai-ryu), who instantly replied: 'The flowers cover the mountain with golden brocade. The waters tinge the rivulets with heavenly blue.' 'Universe is the whole body of Tathagata,' observed Do-gen. 'The worlds in ten directions, the earth, grass, trees, walls, fences, tiles, pebbles—in a word, all the animated and inanimate objects partake of the Buddha-nature. Thereby, those who partake in the benefit of the Wind and Water that rise out of them are, all of them, helped by the mysterious influence of Buddha, and show forth Enlightenment.'"

The Religion of the Samurai; A Study of Zen Philosophy and Discipline in China and Japan (1913)

Nicole
Smile

Amy
Smile

Printed in Great Britain
by Amazon